SPEAKING DOG

Understanding Why Your Hound Howls and Other Tips on Speaking Dog

EDGE BOOKS™

By Tammy Gagne

Consultant:
Jennifer Zablotny, DVM
Member, American Veterinary
Medical Association

CAPSTONE PRESS
a capstone imprint

Edge Books are published by Capstone Press,
1710 Roe Crest Drive, North Mankato, Minnesota 56003.
www.capstonepub.com

Books published by Capstone Press are manufactured with paper
containing at least 10 percent post-consumer waste.

Library of Congress Cataloging-in-Publication Data
Gagne, Tammy.
  Speaking dog : understanding why your hound howls and other tips on speaking
    dog / By Tammy Gagne.
    p. cm. — (Edge books. Dog ownership)
  Includes bibliographical references and index.
  Summary: "Describes information and tips on understanding dogs"—Provided
    by publisher.
  ISBN 978-1-4296-6528-5 (library binding)
  1. Dogs—Behavior. 2. Dogs—Barking. 3. Human-animal communication.
    I. Title.
  SF433.G34 2012
  636.7'0887—dc22

                          2011003792

Editorial Credits
Angie Kaelberer, editor; Bobbie Nuytten and Ashlee Suker, designers;
  Marcie Spence, media researcher; Eric Manske, production specialist

Photo Credits
Alamy Images: Myrleen Pearson, 28, Petra Wegner, 23; iStockphoto: pinkpig,
cover; Minden Pictures: Roger Tidman, 24; Shutterstock: 578foot, 26, Alvaro
Pantoja, 4, Andrey.tiyk, (design element), Blend Images, 17, chudo-yudo,
(design element), Cristi Matei, 1, 22, Dolly, (design element), Eky Studio,
(design element), Elenamiv, (design element), FotoJagodka, 18, HASLOO,
(design element), Inhabitant, 25, Joy Brown, 14, Monika Wisniewska, 19,
Morgan Lane Photography, 11, Nazzu (design element), pixshots, 7, Sergey
Kozoderov, 27, Soundsnaps, 21, Torsten Lorenz, 8, X2Photo, 15, Zoyaa, 12

Printed in the United States of America in Stevens Point, Wisconsin.
122011   006527WZVMI

Table of Contents

CHAPTER 1 Man's Best Friend

Dogs have been part of people's lives for at least 14,000 years. They work alongside people in a variety of jobs. They also serve as loyal companions.

Dogs seem to have an amazing ability to understand people. Sometimes they seem to know what we are feeling even before we do. When we need some fresh air, they are ready for a walk. When we crave quiet time, they cuddle alongside us. It may be this understanding that makes us love our dogs so much.

But how well do we understand dogs? Do we know why they do the things they do? The more we understand our dogs, the easier their care and training will be.

CHAPTER 2
From Wolves to Dogs

Dogs descend from wolves. All breeds from the tiniest Chihuahua to the largest Great Dane can be traced back to the wolf. But wolves are wild animals, while dogs have been **domesticated**.

No one knows for sure how people and wolves first came together. People may have tried to tame wolves for protection or for hunting. Or wolves may have hung around human camps in search of food scraps. Over time, these wolves would likely have become more comfortable around people. Eventually domesticated dogs were living alongside people.

People kept and bred dogs with the best abilities and personalities. This selective breeding went on for thousands of years. As time went on, people realized that dogs also made good companions. They began to keep dogs as pets.

domesticate—to tame an animal

All dog breeds—big and small—
descend from wolves.

Wolf Packs

Today's dogs do share some qualities with wolves. Breeds like the Siberian husky and the Alaskan malamute even look similar to wolves. Another important similarity is pack life.

Wolves live in packs. They hunt, eat, and sleep together. Each pack has a breeding pair. These **dominant** wolves are sometimes called alpha wolves. The alphas are often the oldest healthy wolves in the pack. They are the first ones to eat after hunting. The female alpha chooses the pack's den site when it is time for her to give birth.

Wolves live in social groups called packs.

dominant—being the most powerful member of a group

DOG DATA

Both wolves and dogs have 42 teeth. But a wolf's four canines are much longer than a dog's. They can be up to 2.5 inches (6.4 centimeters) long.

In small packs, the other wolves are usually the offspring of the alphas. When the young wolves are between 1 and 3 years old, they leave to start their own packs.

Large packs may include beta wolves. The betas help the alphas protect the pack. The female beta often helps the alpha female care for the pups.

Omega wolves are last in terms of power. Omegas have the most **submissive** personalities. They avoid conflict whenever possible and may use playful behavior to distract the other wolves from attacks or fights.

submissive—willing to give control to another

Pack Life of Dogs

The dog's pack is the family it lives with. If other dogs live in the house, they also belong to the pack. The alphas are usually the human parents. Children may serve the beta roles, with the dogs acting as fellow betas or omegas. The highest-ranking dog is usually a female.

Like wolves, dogs value their packs. This devotion is the reason many dogs have such a strong **instinct** to protect their owners.

Dogs are social animals that need to spend time with their packs. If left alone too long, a dog may howl like a wolf does when calling for its pack members. A dog that howls or barks constantly is usually trying to tell its human family that it needs more attention.

instinct—natural behavior

A dog considers its human family its pack.

 **DOG DATA**

In 1977 scientists at Ein Mallaha, Israel, discovered the 12,000-year-old remains of an elderly person alongside the bones of a puppy. The person's left hand still rested on the dog's skull.

CHAPTER 3
Your Dog's Five Senses

The things we see, hear, smell, taste, and feel all affect how we view the world. Our senses are like a network of computers that process all the information around us. The same is true for dogs.

The Nose Knows

Smell is a dog's strongest sense. Most dogs' noses have about 200 million **scent receptors**. A human nose has only about 5 million. When you and your dog visit a new place, you probably notice the sights. But your dog first notices all of the smells. Your dog can probably smell a chipmunk long before it runs across your yard.

scent receptor—a cell in the nose that gathers smells

When dogs meet, they sniff each other. If they have met each other before, they recognize each other's scents instantly.

One reason dogs sniff each other is to determine if the other dog is a threat.

DOG DATA

Some dogs have been trained to detect cancerous tumors in people by sniffing the person's skin or breath.

A bloodhound's nose has 300 million scent receptors.

Some dogs use their sense of smell to help people. Search and rescue dogs are trained to follow the scents of missing people. Other dogs use their noses to sniff for illegal drugs. The bloodhound breed is especially known for its scent-finding ability.

Good Listeners

Dogs can hear many sounds that people can't. People can hear sounds up to 20,000 **hertz**. Dogs can hear up to about 60,000 hertz, depending on the breed.

Early dogs used their hearing to find prey. Since their owners provide them with food, today's dogs don't need to hunt. But they use their hearing in many other ways. Some work as hearing dogs for people who are deaf. Pet dogs use their hearing in everyday activities such as obeying spoken commands and playing. There is a reason many dog toys come with squeakers!

DOG DATA

Some dog trainers use dog whistles. People can't hear the high-pitched sounds made by these tools. But they instantly capture a dog's attention.

hertz—a unit measuring sound wave vibrations

Many dogs enjoy a gentle massage with fingers or a dog brush.

A Gentle Touch

Touch is a great way to bond with your dog. But like people, dogs have different personalities. Some dogs enjoy cuddling with their owners. Others prefer to spend time nearby but not touching their owners. If your dog resists being petted, stop at once and give it some space.

Just as touch can show love, it can also communicate bad feelings. Dogs dislike being held against their will. Never hit your dog or punish it in any physical way. You can correct your dog by teaching it verbal commands.

Dogs' eyes sense movement better than people's do.

Sharp Eyes

You may have heard that dogs can only see black and white images. This is a common myth. But dogs do not see as many colors as people do. People's eyes have three kinds of **cones**. Dogs have only two types. A person can see a full range of colors. A dog sees only shades of yellow, gray, and blue.

A dog's biggest visual advantage is its ability to see well in the dark. A dog's eye has more **rods** than a person's eye does. These cells allow the dog to see in very dim light. A dog's eye also has a large pupil that lets in more light than a human pupil does. This night vision is useful to wolves in hunting. It also comes in handy for watchdogs.

cone—an eye cell that senses color
rod—an eye cell that responds to low light

Not Very Tasty

Most dogs love to eat. For this reason, you may think dogs have a strong sense of taste. The truth is that dogs have very limited taste. Dogs have about one-sixth as many taste buds as people do.

With their limited sense of taste, dogs don't need spices or flavorings added to their food to make it more appealing. But most dogs do like some variety in their diet. Healthy foods like raw carrots and cooked chicken make good training treats.

Dogs prefer food with a savory taste, such as meat.

CHAPTER 4

Barks and Body Language

Dogs can't talk. But they are always speaking through their barks and movements. These movements are called body language.

A dog's body language can be difficult to read at times. A wagging tail means a dog is happy and friendly, right? Not always! Short, stiff tail wags can mean that the dog wants to be left alone.

A dog's breed, personality, and training affect how it acts. The best way to know what your dog is feeling is to pay close attention. That way, you'll learn what each of its **gestures** mean.

gesture—an action that shows feelings

Speak, Rover!

Just like body language, each sound a dog makes means something. Quick, high-pitched yaps are usually a friendly hello. Howls that last a long time are often a sign of loneliness. A low-pitched, rumbling growl means the dog feels threatened. Mid-pitched, quick barks alert the dog's owners to something, such as a ringing doorbell.

Dogs bark to communicate both with humans and other dogs.

A play bow means that your dog is ready for some fun.

Happiness

A happy dog bubbles with excitement. Happy dogs open their mouths or bark in an upbeat tone. They also wag their tails in a quick side-to-side motion. A very excited dog may wag its entire backside.

Sometimes a dog will stretch out its body, lower its head, and raise its hindquarters. When your dog does this in front of you, it is inviting you to play. This gesture is called a play bow.

Fear

Dogs also use body language to show fear. A frightened dog pulls its ears back, widens its eyes, and tucks its tail between its legs. Sometimes it will stare at or take a step back from the source of its fear.

A fearful dog may turn angry if it feels cornered.

Rolling on the back can show submission or playfulness.

Submission

When a dog rolls onto its back around a person or another animal, the dog is saying, "You rank higher than I do, and I accept that." Many dogs do this when greeting their owners.

Sadness and Anger

All dogs need rest, but a sad dog spends more time than necessary lying down or sleeping. It may show little interest in playing. Most dogs don't feel sad for long. If your dog acts this way for more than a day or so, call your veterinarian. Your pet could be sick.

Changes in their location or routine can make dogs sad.

Never approach a dog that is acting angry or aggressive.

An angry dog shows several signs. It may stand taller to look as large as possible, holding its tail stiff. It may also growl or raise the hair on the back of its neck. Some angry dogs bark extra loudly. These are all warnings that you should back away at once. Some dogs act aggressively around their food. Others may use angry behavior to protect their homes or loved ones.

Dog "kisses" are similar to how puppies lick their mothers.

Learning from Your Dog

Many people think of their dogs as family members. But owners need to understand that dogs are not people. Dogs have their own ways of seeing the world and reacting to it. The better you understand your dog's behavior, the more enjoyable your life and your pet's life will be.

DOG DATA If you come across a dog that seems angry, don't run! Avoid eye contact with the dog as you turn your body sideways and move slowly away.

Quick Guide to Canine Body Language

	Body	Ears	Eyes	Mouth	Tail
Angry	Standing tall	Forward	Open wide	Teeth exposed	Still or wagging stiffly
Happy	Well-balanced	Natural	Alert	Open, relaxed—may look like a smile	Wagging
Playful	Stretched out	Erect	Friendly	Open, tongue may hang out	Wagging
Relaxed	Still	Natural	Normal shape	Slightly open	Hanging naturally
Scared	Cowering	Back	Cast downward	Closed	Between legs

GLOSSARY

cone (KOHN)—a funnel-shaped eye cell that senses color

domesticate (duh-MESS-tuh-kate)—to tame an animal so that it can live with or be used by humans

dominant (DAH-muh-nuhnt)—being the most powerful member of a group

gesture (JESS-chur)—an action that shows a person or animal's feelings

hertz (HURTS)—a unit for measuring the frequency of sound wave vibrations; one hertz equals one sound wave per second

instinct (IN-stingkt)—behavior that is natural rather than learned

rod (ROD)—a cylinder-shaped eye cell that responds to low light

scent receptor (SENT ri-SEP-tuhr)—a cell in the nose that gathers smells

submissive (suhb-MIH-siv)—willing to give control to another person or animal

READ MORE

Mehus-Roe, Kristin. *The Original Dogs for Kids!*
Irvine, Calif.: BowTie Press, 2007.

Pavia, Audrey, and Jacque Lynn Schultz. *Having Fun with Your Dog.* ASPCA Kids. Hoboken, N.J.: Wiley, 2009.

Payne, Renee, and Jennifer Gladysz. *Be A Dog's Best Friend: A Safety Guide for Kids.* New York: Doggie Couch Books, 2009.

Whitehead, Sarah. *How To Speak Dog.* New York: Scholastic Reference, 2008.

INTERNET SITES

FactHound offers a safe, fun way to find Internet sites related to this book. All of the sites on FactHound have been researched by our staff.

Here's all you do:

Visit *www.facthound.com*

Type in this code: 9781429665285

Super-cool stuff! Check out projects, games and lots more at **www.capstonekids.com**

INDEX